Marriage Guide

The Five principles for making marriage Work

AGNES BAKER

Table of content

Introduction

One cannot simply hope for a successful marriage to occur. All parties involved must put forth a lot of effort, be committed, and have a ton of luck. But it doesn't have to be a chore; your union might even be enjoyable! You will find that when you complete all five principles in this course, you are able to think more deeply about your decisions, behaviors, and, ultimately, your spouse.

Principles for making marriage work

1. Communicate with Your Spouse Effectively

2. Plan the Perfect Date

3. Build the best possible trust.

4. Having the best sex ever

5. Resolve disputes as effectively as possible.

Part One: How to Communicate with Your Spouse Effectively

My honeymoon seems to have happened yesterday. It was both one of my marriage's best and worst periods.

I thought it best because I had just wed my soul mate and was completely smitten with him. Worse, since we couldn't communicate with one another and would get into heated disagreements as a result. On our honeymoon, we got into a loud dispute that got so nasty that security at a five-star hotel had to separate us. True incident

We lost so much of our affection in the translation. Between the screams and the love, we became lost. I once believed there was no hope. I believed that these vehement disagreements were what we were intended for.

When I realized there was a solution, my heart leaped.

Our marriage has now lasted more than 20 years. Yes, we still fight, but despite this, we are not discouraged because we have discovered one of the keys to a happy marriage.

The key is in communication.

A happy marriage depends on open communication. The five practices I've listed below will help you improve communication in your marriage. Each one includes a quick piece of advice on how to get started using the skill right away.

I ask questions.

One strategy for influencing others is to ask more questions than to provide answers. Asking your spouse questions is one of the best ways to build a connection with them. Posing questions demonstrates curiosity and focus. This verbal communication makes it clear to your partner that you value the union.

Asking the correct questions is the key. These questions can be asked this week. What do you love most? What is making your life happy now? What is something about me that you might wish to know? What are your goals for the future? What can I do to support you in realizing your goals?

II. Pay attention to your partner.

A crucial ability is listening. In addition to your capacity to interpret what was said, it requires mental clarity, the absence of bias, and probing questions such "what did you mean when you said___?" Too frequently, one spouse in a marriage will attempt to speak while the other is preoccupied with something else. One of the things that contributes to a successful marriage is the ability to maintain productive dialogue through effective listening.

It's crucial to develop and deliberately practice listening skills with your partner.

Consider practicing the following two things this week:

1. Giving yourself enough time to be there is what presence looks like. You are not multitasking and are therefore fully engaged in the chat.

2. You will understand what is being said more clearly and be more likely to recall the point your spouse is making if you ask for clarification.

III. Provide Clear Feedback

While challenging, this is yet another crucial step in establishing effective communication in your marriage. The first few times you express your genuine views and feelings may not be well received if you have not created an environment where candid feedback is valued. However, you will eventually need to develop a feeling of honest feedback if you are truly committed to creating the healthiest marriage possible.

Giving accurate feedback depends on your willingness to take a chance and embrace your feelings.

Giving clear feedback can be done in the following ways:

1. Requesting the right to express your honest opinions on what you overheard your partner say, "Can I tell you what I'm thinking?" I inquire. or "I truly want to tell you how I feel, but I'm afraid you won't hear me"?

2. Avoid using absolutes. These include phrases like "This is your fault" and "I don't like what you are saying." Make remarks that will allow you to modify your position if necessary or that will allow your feelings to alter over time. There is a chance that you would say, "I think I might be hurt, but I'm not sure; I need more information." or "Do you really mean that? I'm concerned that you might say,"

3.Avoid making accusations.

IV. Establishing feedback loops

All of this is about fostering an environment of open dialogue. I won't go too technical about this, but I will briefly explain how a feedback loop functions.

The first thing is a person. Then, that person (second) encrypts a message (third). The fourth recipient receives the deciphered message, followed by the fifth recipient.

A communication process consists of five straightforward steps. As you can see, each component has the potential to be a point of misunderstanding or improper communication. Understanding each step of the process and checking it when you feel your partner is not hearing you clearly can help you build effective feedback loops.

Married couples frequently have trouble listening to one another. As a result, thoughts and sentiments are transmitted without being heard. It's comparable to going live on a webcast, but the person receiving the message on the other end has poor phone service and cannot completely understand it.

Effective feedback loops can be practiced in the following ways:

1.Say what you mean to say while keeping in mind how the other person could understand you.

2. Inquire of the listener if they comprehend what you are saying, then pay attention to their response.

3. If they don't understand what you said, say it again more plainly. (Pro Tip: Proceed serenely.)

4. When the message is clear, go on to the next assertion.

It's time to consult a counselor if you are unable to gain clarity.

V. Employing nonverbal cues

Non-verbal clues are also an important ability. They need to make eye contact, use their hands to speak, and remain composed. What you just read requires "non-verbal communication" in its entirety. There has been research on how people communicate both verbally and nonverbally, but the results have

been conflicting. We are aware of how important nonverbal communication is. large enough for someone to determine whether you are really paying attention to them.

It's crucial to practice nonverbal communication with your partner.

Consider practicing the following this week:

1. When conversing with one another, keep eye contact.

2. Physical composure entails being aware of your body's language. Crossed arms can indicate that you are not just not taking in the information, but also possibly on the defensive.

3. Analyze any inconsistent behavior. A person may claim to be happy while physically displaying melancholy.

Part Two: How to Plan the Perfect Date

I don't have the time,

I frequently hear this response from people. In our society, the idea that we don't have enough time is ubiquitous. We do, though.

We have plenty of time for the items at the top of our priority list. Our daily, weekly, and monthly calendars are filled with obligations related to relationships, employment, education, sports, and personal activities. Are we prioritizing the appropriate things? That is the question.

You'll find five different suggestions for how to enjoy the best date ever down below. Before you go on your date, you'll need to put some effort into some of the concepts and tasks. Some of the concepts merely need your presence and participation.

Whatever the state of affairs you are presently experiencing with your spouse, keep in mind that you can start building a fantastic connection. You need to start acting and offering sacrifices for the things you hold dear.

Let's start.

I. Make Time.

Making time for your spouse is the best way to, well, make time.

You must set aside time, just as you would for any other significant meeting in your life. One of the ways I've discovered to approach this has been really beneficial to me. Here's what I'm thinking. The most crucial weekly chores that enable me to do my work come to mind when I consider how vital my work is. I almost always realize that I must schedule weekly meetings with the most significant individuals in my organization when I think about this. If that is true in terms of creating a strong work ethic, shouldn't the same be true of my marriage? Yes, it is the answer.

The importance of your marriage in your life is elevated when you find and make time for it. It is beneficial to let your spouse know that you are genuinely interested in them. Choose one to two hours a week to dedicate to being in the moment with your partner. If you have young children at home and are unable to get daycare, choose a time when you can put the kids to bed and have a date at home. Making the time will improve your connection and position you for future dates with your spouse.

II. Have Deep Conversations

Not knowing what to talk about or being in a situation where you don't want to talk is one of the most

awkward situations on a date with your spouse. Things are clearly weird because of the silence. Meaningful conversation can occur when you are willing to overcome your discomfort and go into the heart of the person sitting across from you. This is actually the first step toward establishing emotional connection (intimacy).

Great questions, I've discovered, are the secret to a great conversation.

Sounds simple, yeah? It is simpler than you may imagine, but it will take more work than you might anticipate. Being courteous is the first step to asking smart questions. Do you really think about your partner? Do you give them any thought throughout the day? Do you genuinely care about them? For some people, this comes more naturally, while for others, it doesn't. If you want to see growth in this area of your relationship, create a space that is comfortable for dialogue and begin posing questions. Ask about aspirations and desires. Find out what makes them happy. Request assistance and then begin offering assistance where you can.

III. Have fun with one another.

When did you two last enjoy yourselves? How did you act? How did it affect how you felt? You remember the purpose of your marriage when you are having a good time together. You start to rediscover the passion and love you once had. This is why you should date your spouse and why you should go on the best date ever.

It is possible to have a good time on your date every time. This is due to the fact that having fun does not necessitate being active or moving about. Walks, discussions, and romantic, informal, or formal dates are all possible.

Here are a few concepts:

You may get a sense of what's going on in your neighborhood by conducting a fast Google search for "local activities." You might think about attending a performance or planning a meal. A couple I know make dinner reservations at the same place every week. People adore it! They enjoy themselves and get to know the personnel. What you should focus on is how to make this enjoyable for your spouse. Avoid bringing up subjects on your date that you know will be contentious. For that, schedule a different meeting time. Keep your date private and make the most of the time to get to know each other better.

IV. Make it inexpensive

The nature of the dates might vary. I love it when they are! Invest in expensive clothing. Fun times for everyone! It's fantastic when they are casual! Wear your jammies to bed. Fun times, everyone! Recalling your "why?" is essential in this situation. Exactly why do you date your spouse? Building emotional intimacy is the goal of dating someone in order to get to know them and develop closeness on a personal level. Remember to stay on topic! What matters is emotional closeness and connection.

Making French onion soup at home was a favorite date activity for my husband and me. We were viewing a movie about Julia Child, a well-known American who trained as a French chef and published cookbooks. We didn't have enough money to acquire childcare or eat out at a posh French restaurant while we had four kids who were all at home. We began to consider cooking the meals at home using a French cookbook. We chose a night, put our children to bed, went shopping, cranked on some upbeat music, and then cooked and danced in the kitchen.

The key is for you and your spouse to grow an emotional connection and an intimate relationship with one another. Going for a stroll is a cost-free way to accomplish this.

V. Present Yourself Well

Here, I only want to encourage you to put in some effort. Some of you start planning your wardrobe weeks or even days in advance. Others of you end up tossing something on since you don't know what you'll wear out to dinner or on a walk.

Here, I would advise you to think about your spouse and put some effort into dressing nicely. By doing this, you are expressing to them your continued concern for their feelings toward you. My spouse and I both prefer to smell good for each other, so we both wear perfume and cologne. He makes sure to clip his facial hair because he wants a kiss!

It is not our intention to instill a sense of oppression or obligation, but rather to foster a spirit of mutual service. When we approach our spouses in this manner on our dates, we will more effectively convey our love for them.

Final Reflections

Be innovative. Attempt to help one another. Make an effort for your spouse. Being available to chat with them will demonstrate your love for them. to create a kind and respectful environment. These are the methods that will help you build a romantic connection and have the most memorable date ever.

Part Three: How to build the best possible trust.

The woman entered my office and expressed her worries to me regarding her husband. Later, when we met, the husband expressed some worries about his wife. Do you trust him? This is what I posed to them both. Do you have faith in her? Their responses would determine the direction their marriage would take going forward.

I have five years of experience working with couples. Five years' worth of marital conversations. That entails spending countless hours dealing with challenging circumstances and wading through the oceans of grief and suffering as individuals strive to regain confidence in their interpersonal connections.

By far, one of the most crucial elements of a successful marriage is trust. Without trust, your marriage won't be able to flourish. One of the fundamental building blocks for effective and healthy communication as well as intense sex is trust. Here are five ways to get started on the road to establishing trust in your marriage.

I. Be Genuine and honest

While each of the actions outlined here is necessary, being genuine and honest is by far the most crucial. You must be genuine and honest with yourself and with your partner about yourself if you want to establish trust in your marriage. You need to carry out a few tasks for this. You must be able to look in the mirror and truly see who you are. Most people are unable to achieve this because they refuse to acknowledge their shortcomings. They choose to ignore their problems and tell themselves,

"I'm not perfect, but I'm not that horrible," instead. To be completely honest and genuine with oneself, this is a serious failing.

Avoiding comparisons with or judging oneself against others is being honest with yourself. In actuality, it is about accepting reality. In order to be honest, one must be able to recognize and embrace trust.

You must also be truthful with your spouse. Please let them know if they accomplish something outstanding. Inform them if they make a poor choice. Your spouse values you as a spouse beyond all else. When you're truthful with them, they gain.

The key is to phrase it in a way that will make them most open to hearing what you have to say while also being done in the spirit of love. By doing this, you are fostering an environment of honesty that will permeate all aspects of your marital life.

II. Express Interest

Your partner needs to feel that you are interested in them in order to develop trust in your relationship. I think about my husband a lot throughout the day. I consider what he is doing, where he is working, potential conversation starters, and other things. I used to have all of these feelings at the beginning of my marriage but would never express them to my husband. Instead, I would keep them to myself and only bring up matters that required discussion, such as money or other problems that might arise. By doing this, I kept my husband in the dark about the fact that I was constantly thinking about him; he instead thought I only had negative things to say about him.

Here are several methods for expressing interest:

Listen carefully to what they say while they speak.

Take into account their requirements and make an effort to satisfy them without their asking.

Text or call them. Tell them you are considering them.

Take the initiative to resolve your disagreements when they arise.

The culture of trust in your relationship will start to alter as a result of these four activities, which will require work. Your partner will start to trust you in other ways, which will boost your level of intimacy and emotional closeness.

III. Accept Responsibility

"Declare your regrets!" Sometimes it's positive, other times negative. Of course, the problem is our capacity to accept accountability for our deeds and words.

One of the better metaphors I've come across for marriage is two separate cups that combine to form a marriage. Every cup in the relationship is a different person. Each person must accept responsibility for themselves, and when they do, their cups fill and start to overflow into the marital cup.

Being accountable for your words, deeds, and self includes not blaming others, refraining from whining, knowing what you want and conveying it, and being intentional. These behaviors help us develop a stronger sense of personal accountability for our words and deeds, which builds trust within the marriage.

You'll have both successful and unsuccessful periods in your life. It's alright. You can improve trust if you keep working on this.

IV. Non-Defensive Reactions

Responding non-defensively in the midst of an argument when you're being accused of anything or feel personally attacked is one of the hardest things to accomplish. Being a linguistic ninja while communicating non-defensively is like that. It demonstrates self-mastery, and the result is improved communication in your marriage.

There is no doubt that this is an elite-grade communication skill. It will call for skill and practice.

This appears to be:

Assume accountability for your words and deeds.

observant of your body language.

Control your feelings.

Making no excuses

Beyond the first four, further abilities are required to achieve non-defensive communication. You can hopefully start your journey toward improving the trust in your marriage with the help of the four strategies suggested here. These methods are effective.

V. Demonstrating Empathy

The capacity to comprehend and express another person's feelings is known as empathy. The level of trust in your marriage will significantly increase if you are able to develop empathy.

You must be able to pay attention to your partner when they are sharing in order to demonstrate empathy. This implies that you can demonstrate that you are paying attention as they speak. It also entails being able to identify the feelings your spouse is experiencing. You have the unique capacity to try to sense how they are feeling about a specific circumstance while they are sharing things with you, allowing you to inquire further about their feelings.

When you listen to someone else's perspective on a particular problem, you are demonstrating empathy. Even if you disagree with them on the matter, you must be open to their interpretation of events. You can be more explicit about the matter if they feel as though you have listened to them.

Finally, requesting permission is a fantastic exercise in demonstrating empathy. They might interpret this as you asking them, "Can I share what I heard you say?" or "Are we ready to move forward?" Your spouse will notice that you genuinely want to be in a relationship by asking for permission in this way.

Final Reflections

Establishing trust is the basis of any successful relationship. Gaining and losing trust are both challenging. It is the most crucial element in developing a culture of trust. When you accomplish this, your bond with your partner will be incredibly deeper.

Part Four: Having the best sex ever: How to do it

Even just the word "sex" might cause an emotional response. It can cause controversy, and for good reason. There is a new sexual revolution happening right now. Though not always in the public eye, sexual expression has long been a hot topic. Sex was taboo throughout the Victorian era, which lasted for nearly 60 years. Since Dr. Alfred Kinsey founded sexology, our culture has become more accepting of the way the subject of sex is discussed.

Sexuality is a fascinating subject. The majority of newlywed guys want to learn how to have the best sex ever, while many young women are in a different situation. Frequently, their only goal is to win over their husband.

In actuality, sex is more than just a physical action.

Marriage confers a special, sacred status on the act of sexual encounter. Many couples want to engage in healthy sexual activity, but they are unsure of how to go about doing it. Their general lack of physical health, their emotional distance from one another, their lack of confidence in one another, and their general lack of respect for one another are major sources of conflict.

This book addresses four key topics related to creating a fulfilling sexual connection with your partner. Please note that this book makes the assumption that you or your spouse do not have any medical or mental conditions that would prevent you from having a good sexual encounter. The goal of this is to assist you in creating the environment in which you can have the finest sex ever.

I. Establishing a sincere sexual connection

The first step is to make eye contact! In actuality, a physical relationship goes through various stages. Eye to body contact is the first step in the process, followed by eye to eye, voice to voice, hand to hand, arm to shoulder, arm to waist, mouth to mouth, and finally intercourse.

The fact that a process is underway is the most crucial thing to notice in this situation. Too often, we anticipate sexual closeness in our marriages while paying little attention to the act of physical intimacy. I'd advise you to start with a foot rub.

You must not have any sexual expectations when giving your partner a back or foot rub. This entails acting sacrificially toward your partner. In my opinion, you should also pay close attention to embracing and kissing. I'll explain.

Hugging your partner without any sexual anticipation demonstrates sensitive love and might demonstrate how much you value one another. Kissing is crucial, to finish. Pecks on the cheek to

full-fledged French kissing are all examples of kissing. Kissing is a passionate and private pastime. It will only increase your total level of physical intimacy if you calibrate your kisses for both the tender gesture and the intense passion.

II. Establishing Emotional Intimacy

Many of the entries relating to the question "how to have excellent sex" on Google will focus on building "stronger intimacy." This means that you must develop an emotional bond.

Emotional intimacy is one of the key factors underlying the sexual experience. You will have a better sexual encounter if you can develop a strong sense of emotional intimacy. What then is "emotional closeness"?

Simply said, emotional proximity equates to emotional intimacy. Emotional openness and trust are what define an emotional connection.

The quality of your sexual encounter will increase as you gain your partner's trust and reveal more of your weaknesses. This is due to the fact that sex is not just a bodily sensation.

III. Establishing Trust

Trust yourself implicitly. This point cannot be emphasized enough. Your ability to trust each other will play a key role in determining how your physical and emotional relationship develops. Physical intimacy follows emotional intimacy. This implies that it's crucial for you to be able to emotionally connect with your mate. We can fail to recognize the value of monogamy and emotional stability in contemporary American society, where individuals prize uniqueness and sexual prowess. But I can't emphasize enough how crucial cultivating trust is in terms of creating a fulfilling sexual connection with your partner. Sex is best enjoyed when a solid emotional connection has been made with one person over an extended period of time.

Here, the reasoning is straightforward. Your physical relationship is defined by your emotional connection.

So, how do you go about doing this?

By developing your listening skills, you gain the ability to describe what you hear.

Be dependable. Being stable is a sign of reliability.

"Speak your mind." Passive aggression conveys mistrust.

Again, I cannot emphasize enough how crucial trust-building is.

IV. Respecting one another

One of the things I have stressed to couples over the years is the importance of honoring one another when it comes to your physical relationship with your spouse.

Respect, communication, and mutual regard are all examples of how to honor your spouse.

There is a lot to be said about the assumptions married couples make regarding their partner's sexual expectations. People have a range of experiences before getting married. Some people grow up with the values of purity and abstinence instilled in them. Some people develop in more secular surroundings where promiscuity is praised. While some people have never used pornography, others have been porn addicts since childhood. People have these origins, and they subsequently project their expectations onto their romantic partners. As you could expect, it doesn't turn out very well.

Consider how to show as much respect and regard as you can to your spouse as you begin to create a physically and sexually close relationship. In our hyper-sexualized culture, showing your spouse respect and appreciation appears to mean disobeying societal expectations.

Respect in a sexual relationship is demonstrated through building a trusting and open line of communication with your partner. It seems to be asking them about their comfort level rather than assuming anything.

Finally, respecting and admiring your partner is a key component of respect. Does asking "Does my rationale for and behavior of sexual contact with my spouse dignify or degrade them?" have any practical application? I have attempted to assist couples in considering this. The couple's agreement governs the response to these inquiries. Respect and esteem for one another are demonstrated by taking the time to understand one another.

In conclusion, human sexuality was created to strengthen connections between partners. Sex is a key instrument for fostering intimacy in a relationship in this way. This understanding of sex helps us build stronger relationships and strive for the ideal sex experience.

Part Five: Resolve disputes as effectively as possible.

For a number of reasons, most people learn to avoid conflict as they grow up. A person's ability to understand and engage in conflict depends on a variety of factors, including their ethnic background, cultural traditions, language, and intellectual background. Others virtually seem to thrive in conflict contexts, while some cultural origins are very conflict avoidant.

My husband was raised in homes

that were Italian, Mexican, and Middle Eastern. Everyday conflict was a part of his existence!

Growing up in a multicultural home taught him that some members of the family were very at ease with disagreement, which was one of the joys he encountered. I discovered that, while I was raised in

a different atmosphere, for some people, disputes were an opportunity for a greater and deeper relationship. I was raised in a more traditional American family where confrontation was viewed as a danger. You may probably guess what we talked about when we first got married.

All in all, communication problems are the root cause of conflict. There is a middle ground between the two extremes where healthy communication is possible, no matter how much conflict you are comfortable with. Effective communication can identify the source of tension through listening and asking questions. When you are aware of the issue at hand, you can choose to accept responsibility for it or reject it. Direct action is preferred in this process. By putting the next four strategies into practice, you can start to learn how to quickly and diplomatically resolve conflicts with your spouse.

I. Explain the Conflict

What's the fight about, exactly? The practice of effective communication is crucial to conflict resolution. You must be aware of the source of your angst. By asking clarifying questions like these, you can gain clarity. Where did things start to go south? What were you referring to? What caused the event? How did you get into this predicament? How did the discussion progress?

Have you ever noticed how the topic of discussion can change from something innocent like taking out the garbage to a two-headed monster about how much you detest your in-laws? One thing is certain, though: communication is crucial. It might not have been that way for you, and it might have been something altogether else.

By defining the conflict, you might learn what you are really up against. This technique enables you to determine if you are "really" unhappy about something or whether you simply misheard

something and responded.

Asking clarification questions when you're tense or about to engage in conflict is good practice.

II. Pay close attention.

I can't tell you how many times I've misheard something, taken offense, and then reacted inappropriately. Due to my response, the conversation escalated and eventually turned into an unneeded and nasty argument for my husband. The anguish that comes with disagreement is one of the reasons it has become so challenging for us in our marriages.

We believe that conflict causes suffering, and it frequently does. Conflict causes suffering because poor communication was the foundation of the conflict. Poor transmission and reception quality are simple ways to identify poor communication.

Paying close attention while listening improves

reception by addressing the receiver's quality. When you pay close attention, a technique known as "Active Listening" is used, in which you repeat verbatim what your partner says while also seeking clarification.

Practice asking, "Did you mean to say that?" Keep your mouth shut when you hear something that makes you furious and listen to what your companion has to say.

III. Accept Responsibility

If there has been a lot of disagreement in your marriage, you are aware of how painful it is to have a partner who won't accept responsibility. In fact, accepting responsibility for your part in the disagreement promotes trust in your partnership. When one partner refuses to accept responsibility for what is clearly their problem, trust is lost and a

rift develops.

Some people very readily accept responsibility for their problems, misunderstandings, or transgressions against their relationship, while others do not. It can be very frustrating when opinions differ on this matter. You are urged to think about and explain the advantages of accepting responsibility for your part in the disagreement.

The advantages include strengthening your connection, establishing a safe environment, fostering trust, boosting self-worth, and enhancing compatibility. This is where disagreement may be a powerful relationship-building tool. The advantages of accepting accountability for one's role in a conflict are enormous.

Consider whether you can accept responsibility for anything. If so, what can I say to show that I am taking ownership of this problem?

IV. Reconcile Immediately

Don't go to bed furious, my dear buddy, who had been married for many more years than me, advised me on the day of my wedding. I initially believed that this was some of his own wise counsel. I eventually discovered that this was a Biblical idea, though. Ephesians 4:26 of the Bible advises us not to harbor anger in our hearts.

This idea really does apply to all of our relationships. The application of it in a marital relationship, however, is particularly beneficial because it is our most intimate relationship. This is a fairly straightforward concept. Try your hardest not to harbor resentment.

It's crucial to keep in mind that it's easy to be angry when trying to resolve a dispute. I'm sure you already know that. Given this, it's critical to let your anger go. Bitterness only makes you sick and makes

you dump it out, leaving bitterness inside of you. This resentment erupts onto the people you care about. Therefore, make rapid reconciliation your goal.

Learn: The greatest way to practice reconciliation is to beg for forgiveness on your end before asking, "Where do we proceed from here?" People come together via reconciliation to continue their path.

Finally?

I've gotten better at accepting disagreement with love. I don't like having disagreements with the people I care about, but I do like the way that greater communication, accepting responsibility, and reconciliation work. I try my hardest to keep the people I care about close by. Understanding how to handle disagreement will only benefit and inspire you more.

One of the most fulfilling partnerships you will ever

have is marriage. Put forth every effort to maintain it. Love will flourish as a result, and you will too

Strategies for Keeping Your Partner Engaged

Being in a relationship requires time, dedication, tolerance, the capacity to forgive, openness and vulnerability, as well as the desire to offer without expecting anything in return. Even though it will take a lot of labor, the potential returns will be well worth it. You must make an effort to keep your relationship fresh even as you attempt to improve it. Here are five suggestions to assist you:

1. Try your best to be there.

You could believe that being present simply requires being in the same room as your companion. But in today's world, it's simpler to text than to talk, even when two people are in the same room. Everybody is engrossed with their electronics. Put the gadgets on silent. One approach to keeping your partner interested is by being

physically present, but there is more at stake than merely taking up space.

2. Be simple.

How often have you noticed that you are droning on without ever getting to the point? This tendency is at best irritating and is also bad for relationships. Before you speak, give your words some thought. It's best if you can express it in a single statement. If not, limit yourself to no more than two or three points. This is sufficient to get your point across without boring your spouse.

Relationships require a lot of simplicity. Additionally, if you and your partner have been together for a while, you likely speak in a form of shorthand. Without a lot of additional words, he or she will be able to fill in the spaces and get the general idea.

3. Share your dreams with one another.

Any partnership will spend a

significant amount of time discussing children, household expenses, careers, finances, health, and other issues and responsibilities. It can occasionally appear overwhelming, leaving little time for reflection or taking steps toward goals. Set aside some time to discuss each other's dreams with your partner.

Nothing energizes you more than being honest about what matters to you most. Make sure this is a two-way street, please. Allow your spouse to take the lead to make things simpler. By doing this, you can be sure that you won't talk for an excessive amount of time about your dreams.

4. Small things have a big impact.

One method to keep things new is to do things that surprise and please your spouse if you want them to stay engaged over the long term. It doesn't have to be a pricey present or a fancy supper. Lighten the

load by taking on a duty or making plans for someone to keep the kids so you and your partner may have a glass of wine while the sun sets.

Write brief letters to one another and hide them somewhere that only the two of you will likely see them. This is the modern version of love letters, except it's condensed to the point faster. Your feelings speak louder than your words do. Your companion is compelled to show interest.

5. Make up and kiss.

No matter how difficult your day has been, refrain from venting to your partner. Determine to call a timeout before you go to bed, even when the debate veers into a contentious area and harsh words are spoken. Even if you might not feel like kissing right now, make a point of delaying the conversation until later. Be cordial, welcoming, and respectful of one another. On the other hand,

making up and truly kissing each other is the best way to strengthen your relationship. Follow your best course of action at the time.

www.ingramcontent.com/pod-product-compliance
Lightning Source LLC
LaVergne TN
LVHW020528160826
845677LV00015B/3957

* 9 7 9 8 3 5 8 1 2 5 2 9 2 *